Cambridge Primary

CW00530096

Hodder Cambridge Primary

English

Activity Book

B

Foundation Stage

Ruth Price

HODDER
EDUCATION
AN HACHETTE UK COMPANY

Acknowledgements

Every effort has been made to trace all copyright holders, but if any have been inadvertently overlooked the Publishers will be pleased to make the necessary arrangements at the first opportunity.

Text credits

p.16 The poem *Jelly on a Plate* from *This Little Puffin* compiled by Elizabeth Matterson (Puffin, 1991). Copyright © Elizabeth Matterson 1969, 1991. p.17 The poem *Curry and Rice* from *This Little Puffin* compiled by Elizabeth Matterson (Puffin, 1991). Copyright © Elizabeth Matterson 1969, 1991.

Hachette UK's policy is to use papers that are natural, renewable and recyclable products and made from wood grown in well-managed forests and other controlled sources. The logging and manufacturing processes are expected to conform to the environmental regulations of the country of origin.

Orders: please contact Bookpoint Ltd, 130 Milton Park, Abingdon, Oxon OX14 4SB. Telephone: (44) 01235 827720. Fax: (44) 01235 400454. Lines are open from 9.00–5.00, Monday to Saturday, with a 24-hour message answering service. You can also order through our website www.hoddereducation.com

© Ruth Price 2019

Published by Hodder Education

An Hachette UK Company

Carmelite House, 50 Victoria Embankment, London EC4Y 0DZ

Impression number   5 4 3 2 1

Year   2023 2022 2021 2020 2019

Cover illustrations by Steve Evans

Illustrations by Vian Oelofsen

Typeset in FS Albert Regular 17/19 pt by Lizette Watkiss

Printed in the United Kingdom

A catalogue record for this title is available from the British Library

978 1 5104 5725 6

Contents

Describing position

Use these words to say where things are.

on top of 	under 
next to 	between 

The carrot is **on top of** the sack.　The carrot is **under** the sack.

The carrot is **next to** the sack.　The carrot is **between** the sack and the bucket.

⭐ Name the fruits. Say where they are on the stall. Use these words:

| on top of | under | next to | between |

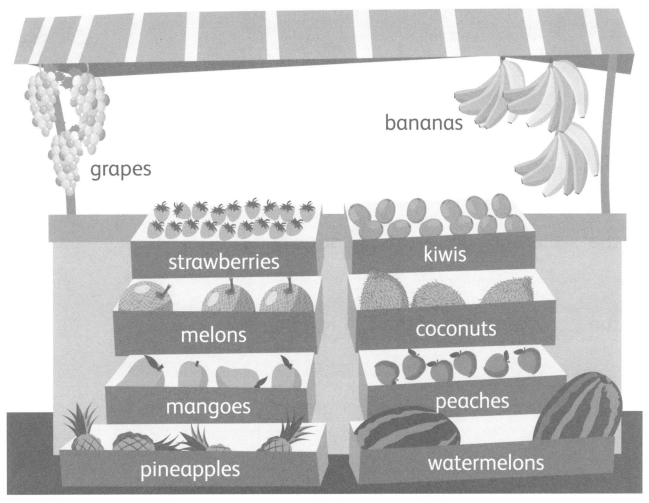

bananas

grapes

strawberries

kiwis

melons

coconuts

mangoes

peaches

pineapples

watermelons

⭐ Ask a question about where the fruits are on the stall.

Begin your question with the word where .

Where are the melons?

The melons are next to the coconuts.

⭐ Talk about the fruit stick using these words:

| on top of | under | next to | between |

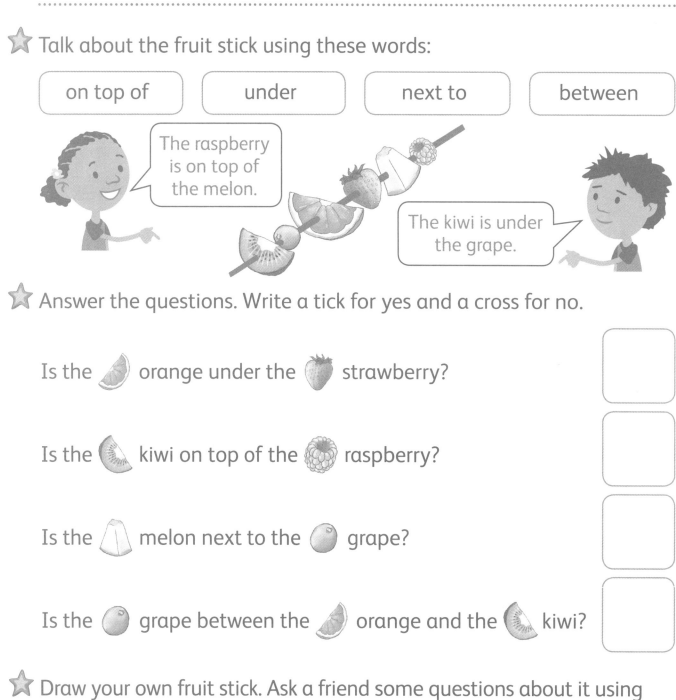

The raspberry is on top of the melon.

The kiwi is under the grape.

⭐ Answer the questions. Write a tick for yes and a cross for no.

Is the 🍊 orange under the 🍓 strawberry? ▢

Is the 🥝 kiwi on top of the 🫐 raspberry? ▢

Is the 🍈 melon next to the 🫐 grape? ▢

Is the 🫐 grape between the 🍊 orange and the 🥝 kiwi? ▢

⭐ Draw your own fruit stick. Ask a friend some questions about it using these words:

| on top of | under | next to | between |

Following instructions

 Name the vegetables. Join the vegetable faces to the matching real vegetables.

 Draw a pizza face. Follow the instructions. Put:

1. for the eyes	4. for the ears
2. for the mouth	5. for the nose
3. for the eyebrows	6. one more vegetable for the hair.

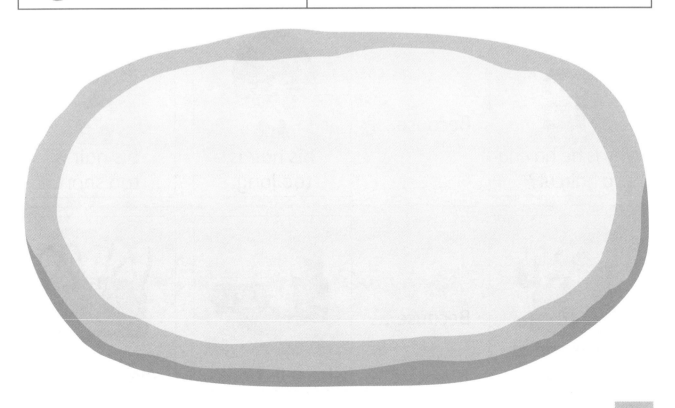

Why and *because*

When a question begins with the word **why**, the answer will usually begin with the word **because**.

Why are we going to the market?

Because we need to get some food.

 Circle the correct answer for these questions.
Say the answer starting with the word **because**.

Why are they in town?

Because …

it is night.

it is market day.

Why is he having a haircut?

Because …

his hair is too long.

his hair is too short.

Why is she at the market?

Because …

she sells books.

she sells bags.

Play this game with some friends. Say these words each time.

I'm going to the market **because** …

Each player adds something new. How many things can you remember?

I'm going to the market **because** … I need a bag.

I'm going to the market **because** … I need a bag and some oats.

I'm going to the market **because** … I need a bag and some oats and a torch.

I'm going to the market **because** … I need a bag and some oats and a torch and a fish.

Word families: musical instruments

⭐ Name the instruments. Join each to its player.

⭐ Name the instruments. Join each to its sound words.

| toot-toot | ting-ting | boom-bang |

| gong | oom-pa | shuka-a-shuka |

Say the names of the instruments. Tell a friend about how to play them.

sleigh bells

clave cubana

tambourine

djembe drum

guiro

bar chimes

xylophone

cymbals

conga drum

 Join the things that are similar. Say why.

11

Retelling a story or an event

⭐ Look at the pictures. Tell what happened.

⭐ Read the sentences together. Number them in the correct order.

Lan hit the shells – bang, bang, bang. It was fun.

Lan was at the market.

Mum got the shells for Lan.

A man was selling shells.

⭐ Have you banged coconut shells to make music? Tell a friend about it.

⭐ How did Lan feel at the market when
she played the coconut shells?
Draw a time when you felt like this.
Tell your story to a friend.

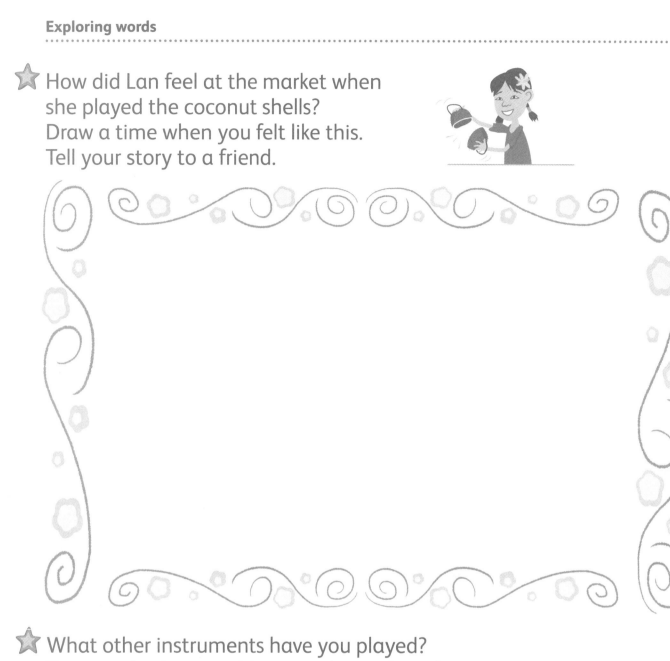

⭐ What other instruments have you played?
Draw and write two things you have played.

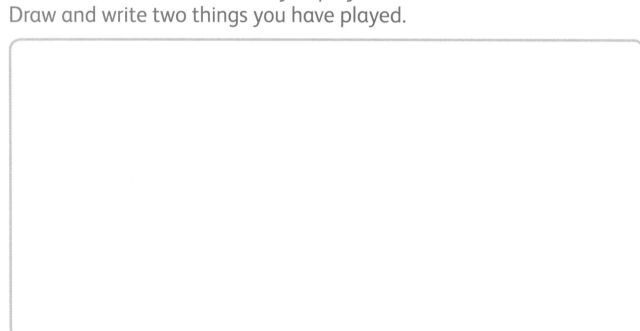

Clapping words

You can clap or tap the rhythm of a word. The number of claps and the way you clap them are the word's rhythm.

The word **maracas** has 3 quick claps. Try it!

ma - rac - as

⭐ Look at each picture. Say its word. Clap the word. Circle the number of claps.

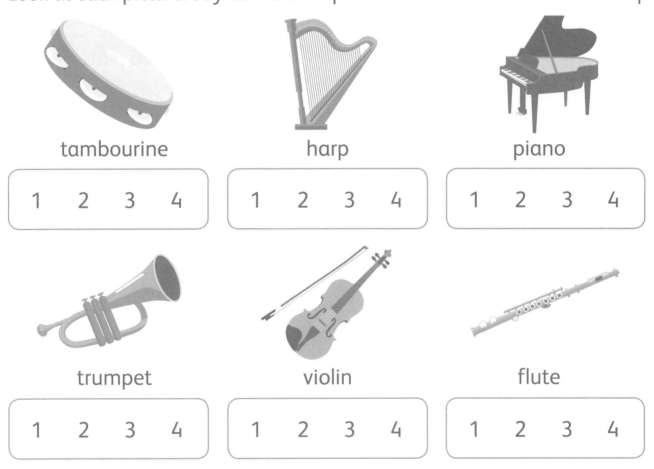

tambourine

| 1 | 2 | 3 | 4 |

harp

| 1 | 2 | 3 | 4 |

piano

| 1 | 2 | 3 | 4 |

trumpet

| 1 | 2 | 3 | 4 |

violin

| 1 | 2 | 3 | 4 |

flute

| 1 | 2 | 3 | 4 |

⭐ Read and clap the phrases. Write a dot for each clap under the words. Join the pairs that have the same number of claps.

off   to   the   market

at   the   farm

in   the   shop

in   the   car   park

Rhythmic poems

 Read these rhymes together.
Clap them.

Jelly on a plate,
Jelly on a plate;
Wibble-wobble,
Wibble-wobble,
Jelly on a plate!

Ice cream on a plate,
Ice cream on a plate;
Slippy-slidey,
Slippy-slidey,
Ice cream on a plate!

 How many claps?

peas = ☐ clap

popcorn = ☐ claps

spaghetti = ☐ claps

16

Read and clap the rhyme on page 16 with these things on the plate.

peas   popcorn   spaghetti

 Read this rhyme. Clap it.

Curry and rice,
Curry and rice,
Everybody here likes
Curry and rice.
We eat it all day,
Never throw it away;
We all like
Curry and rice.

By Elizabeth Bennet

 How many claps?

curry and rice = ☐ claps

Clap the words for each picture.
Tick the things with the same rhythm as **curry and rice**.

chicken and chips

pineapple

pizza and peas

noodles in a bowl

jelly and cream

bananas in a bowl

 Say the rhyme on page 17 again with the things you have ticked.

 Draw something that has the same rhythm as these things.

pineapple

cookies on a plate

doughnut

Laugh out loud

A nonsense rhyme is often a funny or silly rhyme.

Chop chop

Chop, chop, choppity-chop,
Cut off the bottom,
And cut off the top.
What there is left we will
Put in the pot;
Chop, chop, choppity, chop.

By Anonymous

 Read this nonsense rhyme together!

Peas

I eat my peas with honey,
I've done it all my life.
It makes the peas taste funny,
But it keeps peas on the knife.

By Anonymous

19

Say the rhyme on page 19 again. Don't say **peas**, say …

rice

seeds

corn

 Now you choose a food to add to the rhyme.
Write the word for your food on each line. Read your rhyme to a friend.

_____

I eat my _____ with honey,

I've done it all my life.

It makes the _____ taste funny,

But it keeps _____ on the knife.

Phoneme spotting

These letters have just one sound.

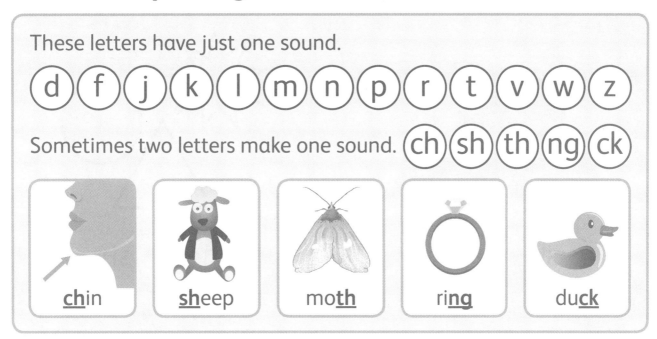

d f j k l m n p r t v w z

Sometimes two letters make one sound. ch sh th ng ck

| chin | sheep | moth | ring | duck |

⭐ Say the word for each picture. Tick the things that begin with sh .

Circle the things that begin with ch .

Circle the letters that begin the word for the picture.

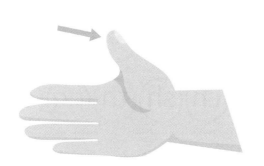

sh   th

ch   sh

sh   ch

th   sh

ch   th

ch   th

Say the word for each picture.

Tick the things that end in ck. Circle the things that end with ng.

 Circle the letters that end the word for the picture.

ck ng	ck th

ng   sh

th   ng   ck   sh   ck   ch

The alphabet: letter sounds and names

This is the alphabet. Each letter has a sound and a name.

a b c d e f g h
i j k l m n o p
q r s t v w x y z

Can you say the sound and name for each letter in the alphabet?

 Read this alphabet song using the letter names. Say it or sing it!

a-b-c-d-e: Will you play with me?

f-g-h-i-j: Do you want to play?

k-l-m-n-o: Let's go, go, go!

p-q-r and s: We are the best.

t-u-v and w: What shall we do?

x-y and z: Oh no! It's time for bed.

Make a food alphabet chart. Say the sound and name for each letter. Draw a food in the blank boxes. It must begin with the letter sound.

a is for	b is for	c is for	d is for
apple			doughnut
e is for	f is for	g is for	h is for
egg		grapes	horned melon
i is for	j is for	k is for	l is for
ita palm		kiwi	
m is for	n is for	o is for	p is for
q is for	r is for	s is for	t is for
quince	radish	sapodilla	taco
u is for	v is for	w is for	x is for
ugli fruit	vine leaf		box of cherries
y is for	z is for		
	zucchini		

Z is for zucchini!

Tricky words

Some words are tricky to read. Try to read them in these groups.

no	go	you	to	the	was

he	she	we	me	be

 Fill each gap with a tricky word from the box above.

We _____ to the market on the bus.

_____ go _____ the shops on foot.

_____ is my mum and _____ is my dad.

Meet _____ in town at the boat.

It will _____ a hot day.

It _____ night and _____ moon was bright.

Reading signs

Signs give us information at school. They tell us about things in words and pictures.

 Read the signs together. Join each word sign to its matching picture sign.

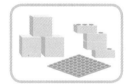

| book corner |

| dressing up |

| art corner |

| bricks and construction |

| small world |

 Draw and write a new sign for your classroom.

Signs give us information outside too. They tell us about things in words and pictures.

 Read the signs together. Join each word sign to its matching picture sign.

 traffic lights

street crossing

roundabout

no cycling

planes

people walking

Draw and write a new sign for your street or town.

Sorting books

There are lots of different kinds of books.
Some books tell stories. Some books give information.

story book

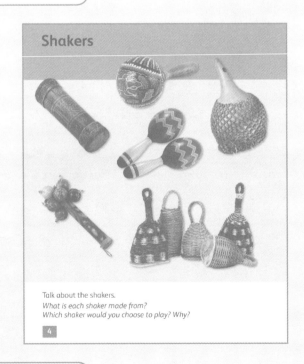

information book

Sort the story books and the information books.
Join each book to the correct shelf.

The king's walk

Park in the dark

Vans and cars

The sun and the moon

Chicken's big day out.

story books

information books

Things with Wings

How rabbit lost his tail

A big book of songs

⭐ Draw a story book cover that you like.

⭐ What is the story book about? Why do you like it?

_____

_____

⭐ Draw an information book cover that you like.

⭐ What is the information book about? Why do you like it?

_____

_____

Following instructions

⭐ Read how to make a shaker. The order is mixed up. Number the steps in order.

Shake the pot…
shuka-shuka!

Stick fun things on
the pot.

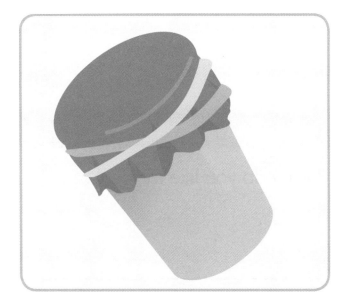

Fix the card tight on
top of the pot with
some bands.

Get a pot. Put seeds
in the pot.

Tick two things you would like to make.
Say how you could make these things.

Happy birthday!

5

Writing patterns

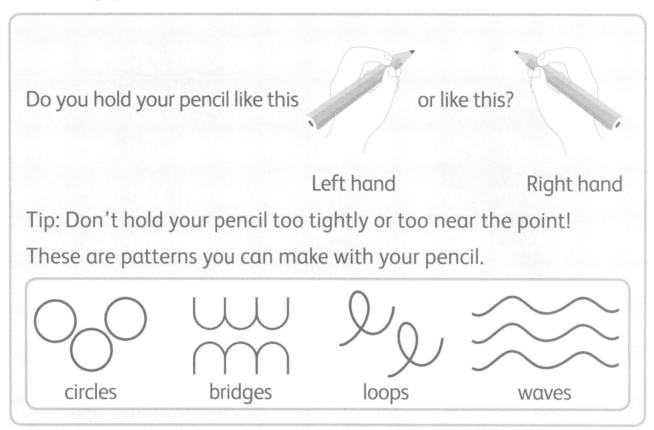

Do you hold your pencil like this   or like this?

Left hand   Right hand

Tip: Don't hold your pencil too tightly or too near the point!

These are patterns you can make with your pencil.

circles   bridges   loops   waves

 What patterns can you see in the picture? Tell a friend.

Trace these patterns with your finger.
Then trace them with your pencil.

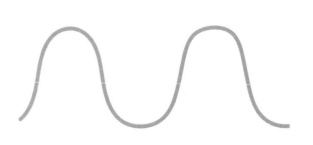 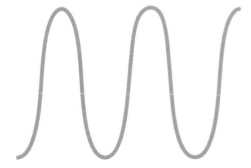

37

Writing lower case letters

Get set to write well:

1. sit up

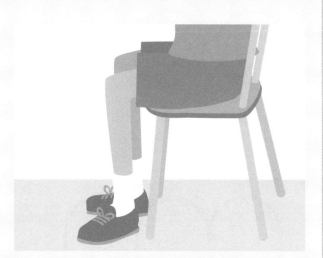

2. feet down and flat

3. elbows off the table

4. chair legs all down

5. do not hold pencil too tightly

6. pencil down and now begin.

Look at how to write each letter. Trace and then copy.

a   b   c   d   e

f   g   h   i   j

k   l   m   n   o

p   q   r   s   t

u   v   w

x   y   z

Writing words and captions

⭐ Change a letter. Write the new word.

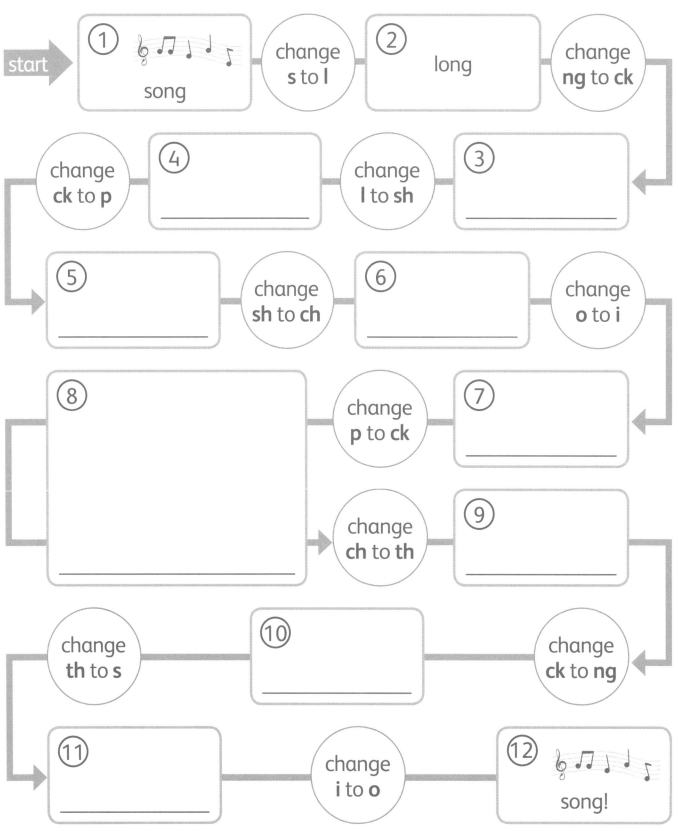

⭐ Draw the picture in box 8.

Sometimes we write two letters to make one sound.

These letters join up to make one sound too.

 ⟶ r**ai**n ⟶

ee ⟶ b**ee** ⟶

igh ⟶ l**igh**t ⟶

oa ⟶ b**oa**t ⟶

These two letters can make two different sounds.

 ⟶ m**oo**n ⟶

oo ⟶ b**oo**k ⟶

Writing

⭐ Say the word for each picture. Write the letters for each sound in the word.

Write a caption for each picture.

What can you remember?

⭐ Read and draw.

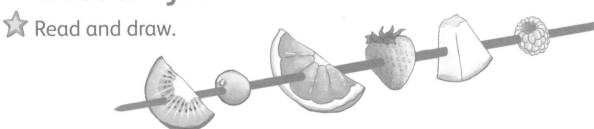

Draw a strawberry on top of a 🥭 melon.

Draw a 🫐 grape under a 🍓 strawberry.

Draw an orange next to a 🥝 kiwi.

Join the things that are the same.

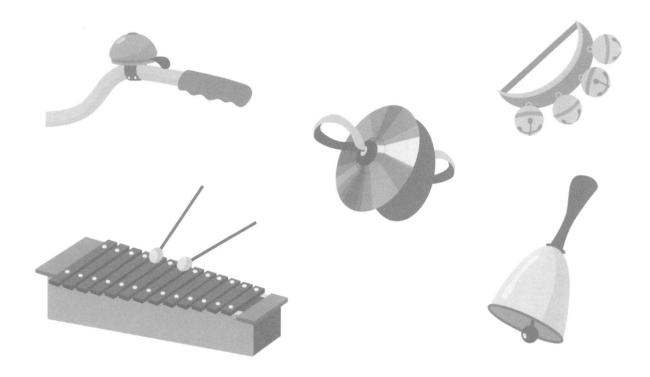

Why are they the same? Tell a friend.

 Say the name of the instrument. Clap the rhythm.
Join the pairs that have the same rhythm.

pi-an-o

trumpet

drum

piano

flute

maracas

trombone

Name each picture. What letter sound is the same in each?
Write the letters.

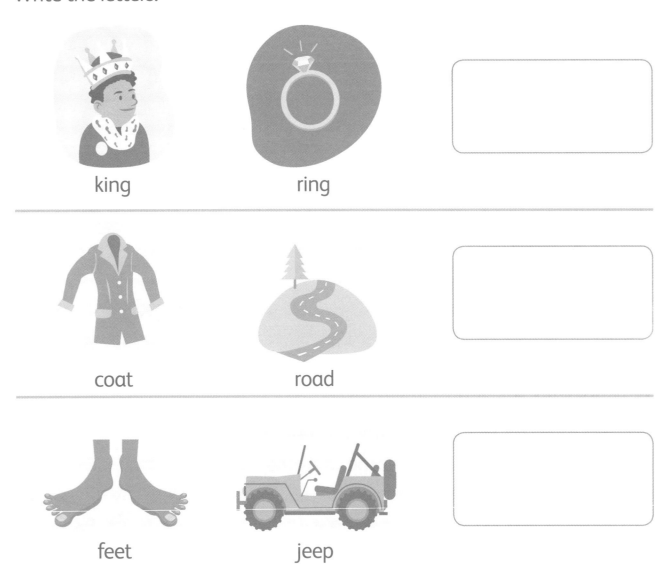

king   ring

coat   road

feet   jeep

 Number the pictures in the correct order to make a sandcastle!

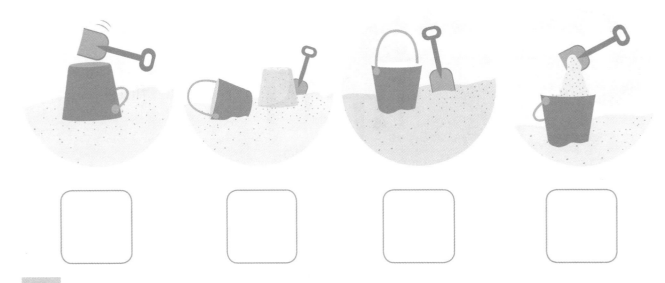

Write a word for each picture.

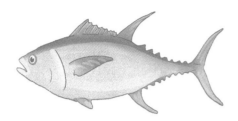

_____ _____

_____ _____

_____ _____

Self-assessment

Colour the stars to show what you can do!

Understanding, listening and speaking	I can describe where things are.	☆
	I can follow instructions.	☆
	I can use *why* and *because*.	☆
Exploring words	I can learn and use new words about musical instruments.	☆
	I can describe the sounds made by instruments.	☆
	I can retell something that happened.	☆
Tuning in to sounds and rhythm	I can clap a rhythm.	☆
	I can hear and repeat rhythms.	☆
	I know when something is funny.	☆
Letters and sounds 2	I can spot phonemes that have two letters, like *sh* and *ng*.	☆
	I know the alphabet letter sounds and names.	☆
	I can read and write some tricky words.	☆
Reading for information	I can read signs in pictures and words.	☆
	I can sort books into story and information books.	☆
	I can read to find out about things.	☆
Writing	I can copy and write patterns with circles, bridges, loops and waves.	☆
	I can write lower case letters in the correct way.	☆
	I can write two letters for one sound, like *th* and *ai*, in words and captions.	☆